For my beautiful mother-
I miss you everyday.

Patterns by Design
A Little Snail Explores Creation
Published by In-De and Friends Media, 2025

Text Copyright © 2025 Billie J York
Illustrations Copyright © 2025 Billie J York

Printed in the USA.

All the characters in this book are fictitious, and any resemblance to actual
persons living or dead is purely coincidental.

All rights reserved. No part of this publication may be reproduced, distributed,
or transmitted in any form or by any means, or stored in a database or retrieval system,
without the prior written permission of the copyright holder.

All inquiries should be directed to
info@in-deandfriends.com

Paperback-ISBN 979-8-9996401-0-9
Hardcover- ISBN 979-8-9996401-1-6

Patterns by Design
A Little Snail Explores Creation

written and illustrated by
Bille J York

Snail Shell Spiral

"Hi, I'm In-De."

Round and round, my shell grows in a gentle spiral.

It keeps me safe while I explore the universe.

"Come with me- let's see what else we can find!"

Sunflower's Center

Look Closely!

In the heart of the sunflower, the seeds swirl into spirals—

each one in just the right place.

Tornado Whirl

A tornado spins in a swirling spiral.

The wind dances-
   round
      and
         round
           and
             round.

Milky Way Galaxy Spiral

The Milky Way is our home in space-

    a swirling spiral of shining stars.

Fingerprint Spirals & Whorls

Look at your fingertip.

Your fingerprint holds tiny spirals and whorls.

No two are exactly the same!

Tree Ring Circles & Whorls

A tree's rings grow in circles and whorls- marking its years layer by layer.

Just like your fingerprint each tree has its own design.

Honeycomb Hexagons

Bees build their honeycombs with strong hexagons.

Each one fits perfectly, side by side-
 a perfect pattern
that holds their golden treasure.

Turtle Shell Hexagons

A turtle's back is covered with special plates-

strong shapes like hexagons that keep it safe.

Snowflake Fractal

Snowflakes grow in repeating shapes called fractals.

Each one is delicate - and completely unique.

Their sides match in perfect harmony.

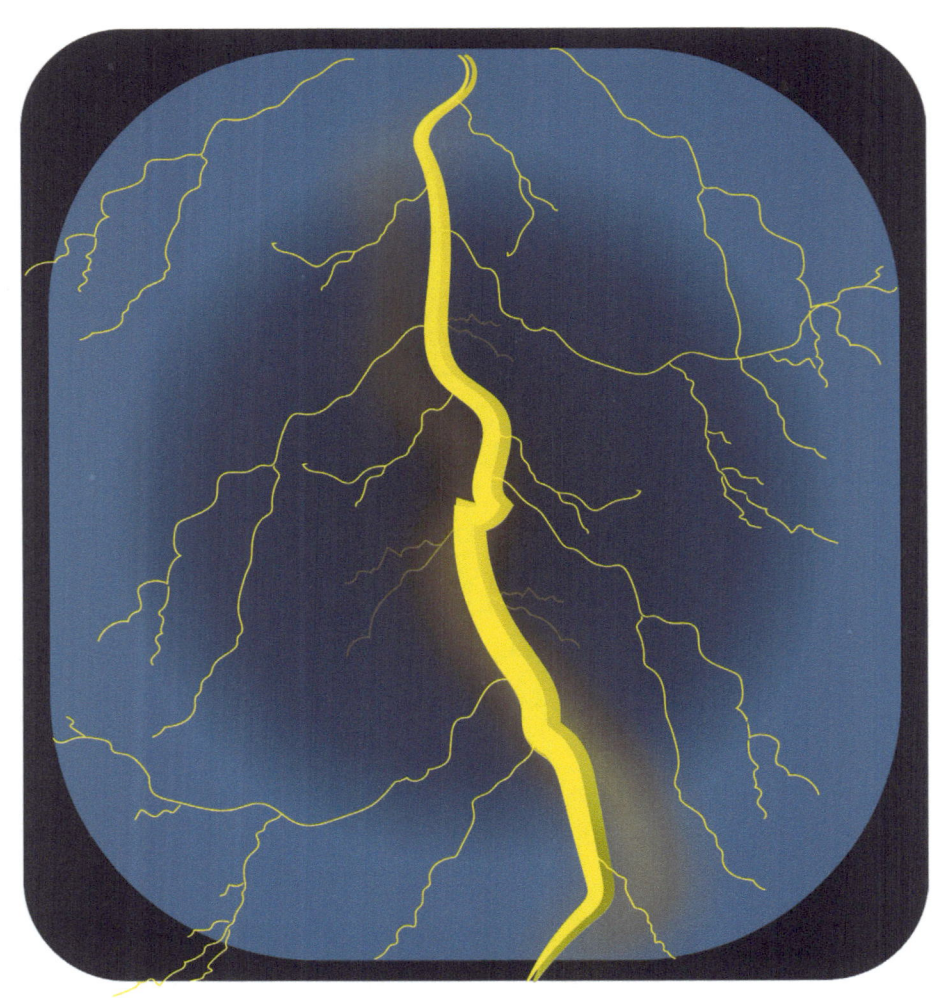

Lightning Fractal

Lightning flashes in branching, repeated lines called fractals.

Even storms show a pattern of design!

In-De's Spirals

Sunflower Spirals

Tornado Spirals

Milky Way Galaxy Spirals

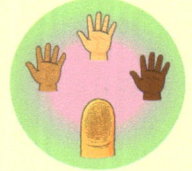
Fingerprint Spirals & Whorls

Tree Ring Circles & Whorls

Honeycomb Hexagons

Turtle Shell Hexagons

Snowflakes Fractals

Lightning Bolt Fractals

Creation's Wonders

Patterns are all around us
in the things
big and small!

They remind us of the
amazing ways God
designed us all!

ABOUT THE AUTHOR

Hi! I'm Billie J York, and I created In-De and Friends to help children discover God's general revelation-the incredible patterns and design found in us and throughout nature. These wonders aren't random; they're part of a purposeful creation that reflects beauty, order, and intention.

Through each page, I hope to awaken curiosity and a sense of wonder in young hearts-encouraging them to keep asking questions, noticing the world around them, and exploring with purpose.

You can find more stories, activities, and resources at www.in-deandfriends.com.

A WORD BY THE AUTHOR

Did you enjoy this book? A quick review on Amazon would mean the world! Your kind words help more families find In-De and Friends. Thank you so much for your support.

"The heavens declare the glory of God,
and the sky above proclaims his handiwork."
- Psalm 19:1 (ESV)